Advanced RAG Techniques Made Simple:

Go Beyond Basic Retrieval and Master the Fundamentals of AI with Retrieval-Augmented Generation (RAG)

Robert C. Miller

TABLE OF CONTENTS

Chapter 1: Introduction to Retrieval-Augmented Generation (RAG)

Hey there! Welcome to the world of RAG, which stands for Retrieval-Augmented Generation. Think of it as a super-powered system that combines two key skills: finding information and using it to create helpful responses. In this chapter, we'll unpack what RAG is all about and why it's so exciting.

1.1 Understanding the Core Concepts of RAG (Information Retrieval and Text Generation)

RAG, which stands for Retrieval-Augmented Generation, is a powerful AI technique that combines two foundational skills: information retrieval (IR) and text generation (TG). Let's break down these concepts to understand how they work together in RAG:

Information Retrieval (IR): Your Super-powered Librarian

Imagine a librarian with superhuman information-finding abilities. This librarian, represented by the IR component of RAG, can wade through massive amounts of text data - articles, code, webpages - to find exactly what you're looking for. When you ask a question, IR goes into action, sifting through this data to identify the documents that hold the most relevant information to answer your query.

Here's a simplified example of how IR might work:

- You ask: "What is the capital of France?"
- IR scans through a vast collection of text documents, searching for keywords like "capital" and "France."

- It finds a document that says: "Paris is the capital of France."
- Bingo! IR has retrieved the relevant information to answer your question.

Technical Note: In reality, IR goes beyond just keyword matching. It often uses sophisticated techniques like semantic search to find documents that have similar meaning even if they don't contain the exact keywords you used in your query.

Text Generation (TG): The Creative Writing Genius

Now, let's introduce the TG component of RAG. Think of it as a creative writing genius who can take the information retrieved by IR and use it to craft a response in a way that's informative and helpful.

Here are some examples of what TG can do with the information IR provides:

- **Answer your question directly:** "Paris is the capital of France."
- **Provide a summary of the retrieved information:** "The document retrieved indicates that Paris is the capital of France."
- **Go beyond a simple answer and offer additional context:** "Paris has been the capital of France since the Middle Ages and is

a major center for art, culture, and fashion."

Putting it All Together: The RAG Magic

The magic of RAG happens when IR and TG work together. IR goes on a hunt for the most relevant information, and TG transforms that information into a comprehensive and informative response tailored to your specific needs. This is what makes RAG so powerful - it leverages the strengths of both information retrieval and text generation to deliver exceptional results.

In the next sections, we'll delve deeper into how IR and TG work together within the RAG framework, and explore some of the intriguing applications of this revolutionary technology.

1.2 Benefits and Applications of RAG: A Game Changer Across Fields

RAG's ability to marry information retrieval with text generation unlocks a treasure chest of benefits that can be applied in various fields. Let's explore some of the key advantages and see how RAG is making waves in different industries:

Benefits of RAG:

- **Enhanced Accuracy:** Unlike some AI systems that might make up information (hallucinate), RAG relies on real-world data retrieved by IR. This significantly reduces the risk of getting inaccurate or misleading answers.

- **Improved Context:** IR goes beyond just finding information; it considers the surrounding text to understand the context of your query. This allows TG to generate responses that are more relevant and on point, addressing the specific intent behind your question.

- **Domain Expertise:** RAG can be a fast learner! By incorporating specialized knowledge bases relevant to a particular field, RAG can be fine-tuned to become an expert in that domain. Imagine a medical chatbot that leverages RAG to answer your health questions based on medical journals and research papers - pretty cool, right?

Applications of RAG in Action:

- **Question Answering Systems:** Ever used a chatbot or virtual assistant that seems a little clueless sometimes? RAG can supercharge these systems by enabling them to answer your questions with greater accuracy, detail, and even provide contextual follow-up questions for clarification.

- **Search Engines Evolved:** Picture a search engine that doesn't just throw a bunch of links at you but actually understands your query and provides a concise answer directly on the search results page. That's the potential of RAG in search engines - simplifying your search journey!

- **Content Creation on Steroids:** Writer's block? No problem! RAG can assist with various content creation tasks. Imagine needing to write a product description, but lacking inspiration. RAG can help by finding relevant information about the product and suggesting creative ways to present it in your writing.

Beyond these examples, the potential applications of RAG are constantly expanding. Researchers are exploring its use in areas like:

- **Machine translation:** Imagine translating a complex document while preserving its meaning and nuances. RAG can help bridge the language gap by providing more accurate and contextually relevant translations.

- **Automatic summarization:** Ever get overwhelmed by lengthy reports or articles? RAG can generate concise summaries that capture the key points, saving you valuable time.

- **Creative Text Generation:** While RAG isn't a novelist just yet, it can be used to generate different creative text formats. Think of it as a brainstorming partner who can help you spark ideas for poems, stories, or even marketing copy.

As you can see, RAG is a versatile technology with the potential to revolutionize the way we interact with information and create content across various fields. In the next chapters, we'll delve deeper into the inner workings of RAG, explore advanced techniques, and unveil the exciting future possibilities this technology holds.

1.3 A Historical Perspective: The Rise of RAG on the Shoulders of AI Giants

RAG isn't a sudden invention, but rather the culmination of exciting advancements in Artificial Intelligence (AI). Here's a whistle-stop tour through time to see how RAG came to be:

The Foundation: Powerful Language Models (LLMs)

Imagine a super-smart writing assistant that can whip up all sorts of creative text formats, from poems to code. These are LLMs, and they laid the groundwork for the text generation (TG) part of RAG. In the early 2010s, researchers made significant progress in LLMs, like GPT-3, which demonstrated the ability to generate human-quality text. This was a crucial first step, as it showed the potential for AI to not just understand information but also create new text formats based on that understanding.

The Retrieval Revolution: Beyond Keywords

While LLMs were busy with text generation, the field of information retrieval (IR) was undergoing its own transformation. Traditionally, IR relied on keyword matching, which could be inaccurate and limited. But then came the rise of semantic search in the late 2010s. This new approach allowed IR systems to not only find keywords but also understand the meaning behind those words and their relationships to each other. This was a game-changer for IR, as it enabled systems to find more relevant information even if the exact keywords weren't used in the query.

The Marriage of Minds: Birth of RAG

Now, let's get to the exciting part! In the early 2020s, researchers saw the potential in combining the strengths of LLMs and semantic search. They brought together the powerful text generation capabilities of LLMs with the improved information retrieval of semantic search, and voila! RAG was born. This marriage of minds created a system that could not only find relevant information but also use it to generate informative and comprehensive responses.

Here's a quick timeline to summarize the journey:

- **Mid-2010s:** Powerful LLMs like GPT-3 emerge, showcasing the potential for AI-powered text generation.

- **Late 2010s:** Semantic search revolutionizes IR, enabling retrieval based on meaning and context, not just keywords.
- **Early 2020s:** Researchers combine LLMs and semantic search, giving birth to the groundbreaking RAG framework.

RAG is still a young technology, but it's rapidly evolving. In the next chapters, we'll explore how RAG works under the hood, delve into some of the advanced techniques being developed, and discover the exciting future possibilities that lie ahead for RAG and its impact on various fields.

Chapter 2: Understanding the RAG Workflow

RAG might seem complex, but don't worry, we'll break it down step-by-step! Think of RAG as a two-part process: information retrieval (IR) and text generation (TG). Let's peek behind the curtain and see how each part works together to create those informative responses.

2.1 A Step-by-Step Breakdown of RAG Processing

Let's say you ask RAG a question. Here's what happens behind the scenes:

1. **Understanding Your Question:** First things first, RAG needs to understand what you're after. It carefully analyzes your question to grasp its intent. What information are you looking for? Are you seeking a simple answer, a detailed explanation, or something else entirely?

2. **IR in Action: The Hunt for Information:** Now, the IR component springs into action. It

utilizes powerful search techniques (like semantic search we discussed earlier) to scour through a vast collection of text data. Think of it as searching through a giant library, but instead of flipping through pages, IR uses clever algorithms to find the documents most relevant to your question.

3. **Extracting the Good Stuff:** Once IR locates the most relevant documents, RAG doesn't just copy and paste everything. It uses information extraction techniques to identify the key passages and information that directly address your query. Imagine highlighting

the important parts of a book - that's what information extraction does, but in a much more automated way.

4. **Crafting a Response with TG:** Now it's TG's turn to shine! Using the information extracted by IR, TG constructs a response that's informative, relevant, and tailored to your specific question. This could be a simple answer, a detailed summary, or even a creative text format depending on the situation!

Here's a simplified Python code snippet to illustrate a basic RAG-like process (remember, this is just an example):

Python

```python
def rag_light(query, documents):

    # Step 1: Analyze the query (omitted for simplicity)

    # Step 2: Information Retrieval (simplified)

    relevant_documents = []

    for document in documents:

        if query in document:  # Basic keyword matching (can be improved)


            relevant_documents.append(document)

    # Step 3: Information Extraction (simplified)
```

```python
    extracted_info = []

    for document in relevant_documents:

        # Imagine a function to find key info in
the document related to the query


        extracted_info.append(find_key_info(document, query))

        # Step 4: Text Generation (simplified)

        response = "Based on the information retrieved, here's what I found: " + str(extracted_info)

        return response


# Example usage
```

```
query = "What is the capital of France?"

documents = ["Document 1: Paris is the
capital of France",

    "Document 2: The Eiffel Tower is
a famous landmark in Paris",

    "Document 3: London is a large
city in England"]


answer = rag_light(query, documents)

print(answer)   # Output: Based on the
information retrieved, here's what I
found: ['Paris']
```

This is a basic example, of course. In reality, RAG uses much more sophisticated techniques for IR and TG. But hopefully, this gives you a good starting point to understand the overall process.

In the next sections, we'll delve deeper into the specifics of IR and TG within RAG. We'll explore advanced search strategies, information extraction techniques, and how prompt engineering helps craft informative responses. Buckle up and get ready to learn more about the magic behind RAG!

2.2 Deep Dive into the Retrieval Component: Search Strategies and Information Extraction

Remember IR, the super-powered librarian from the previous chapter? Here's where we get into the nitty-gritty of how IR hunts down the most relevant information for RAG. Buckle up, because IR has some impressive tricks in its arsenal!

Search Strategies: Beyond Simple Keyword Matching

Imagine searching for a book in a library. Sure, you could just look for the title, but wouldn't it be better to consider the author, genre, or even keywords from the book description? That's the philosophy behind IR's search strategies, which go beyond basic keyword matching:

- **Keyword Matching:** This is the bread and butter of traditional search. IR scans documents for keywords present in your query. While simple, it can be limited, especially if synonyms or related concepts aren't used.

- **Semantic Search: Understanding the Meaning:** This is where things get interesting. IR doesn't just look for keywords; it tries to understand the meaning behind them and their relationships to each other. Think of it like grasping the context of your query. This allows IR to find documents that discuss similar concepts even if they don't use the exact words you used.

Here's an example:

- **Query:** "Best laptops for students"
- **Keyword Matching (Limited):** IR might find documents mentioning "laptops" but not necessarily targeted towards students.
- **Semantic Search (Powerful):** IR can understand the context and find documents discussing student-friendly laptops, even if the

exact phrase "laptops for students" isn't used.

- **Ranking Algorithms: Putting the Best Foot Forward:** IR doesn't just throw any document your way. It uses ranking algorithms to prioritize the most relevant documents. These algorithms consider various factors, like:
    - **Keyword Density:** How many times your keywords appear in the document.
    - **Document Context:** Does the document discuss the topic in a relevant way, or is it just a passing mention?

○ **Document Authority:** Is the document from a credible source?

Information Extraction: Highlighting the Key Points

Once IR locates the most relevant documents, it's not done yet. Imagine finding a bunch of books in the library but not knowing which pages have the information you need. That's where information extraction comes in:

- **Identifying Key Passages:** IR uses techniques to pinpoint the specific sentences or paragraphs within the retrieved documents that directly address your query or provide the most relevant information.

- **Named Entity Recognition (NER):** This fancy term basically means identifying important entities mentioned in the documents, like people, locations, or organizations. This can be helpful, especially for complex queries.

Here's a code snippet (Python) to illustrate a very basic information extraction process (remember, this is a simplified example):

Python

```python
def extract_info(document, query):
```

```python
    # Identify sentences containing query
keywords

    relevant_sentences = []

    for sentence in document.split("."):

        if query in sentence:

            relevant_sentences.append(sentence)

    # Return the first relevant sentence (can
be improved)

    return relevant_sentences[0]


# Example usage
```

```
document = "Paris is the capital of
France. It is a beautiful city with a rich
history."

query = "capital of France"

extracted_info = extract_info(document,
query)

print(extracted_info)   # Output: Paris is
the capital of France.
```

In the next section, we'll explore the other half of the RAG team: Text Generation (TG). We'll see how TG takes the information extracted by IR and uses it to craft informative and helpful responses.

2.3 Exploring the Generation Component: Prompt Engineering and Crafting Informative Responses

We've seen how the information retrieval (IR) component acts as RAG's super-powered librarian, finding the most relevant information to answer your questions. Now, let's meet the other half of the dream team: text generation (TG). Think of TG as the creative writer who takes the information extracted by IR and uses it to craft informative and engaging responses.

Prompt Engineering: Guiding TG in the Right Direction

Imagine giving a writer instructions for a story. In the world of RAG, these instructions are called prompts. Prompt engineering is the art of crafting prompts that guide TG towards generating the kind of response you desire.

Here are some key things to consider when crafting prompts for RAG:

- **Task Specification:** Clearly define what you want TG to do. Do you want a summary of the retrieved information, a direct answer to your question, or something more creative?

- **Information Integration:** Incorporate the information extracted by IR into the prompt. This helps TG understand the context and focus the response on the relevant details.

- **Style and Tone:** Depending on the situation, you might want the response to be informal, formal, humorous, or something else entirely. You can use keywords or stylistic cues within the prompt to nudge TG in the desired direction.

Here's an example of how prompt engineering can influence the response:

- **Query:** "What is the capital of France?"
- **Basic Prompt:** "Generate text about France." (This is vague and could lead to irrelevant responses)
- **Improved Prompt:** "Based on the retrieved information, answer the question: 'What is the capital of France?'" (This is more specific and guides TG towards providing a direct answer)
- **Creative Prompt:** "Write a short poem about the beauty and history of Paris, the capital of France." (This takes a creative approach using the extracted information)

Crafting Informative Responses: Beyond Simple Templates

TG isn't just about copying and pasting information. It can use the extracted information in various ways to craft informative responses:

- **Answering Questions Directly:** When your query has a clear answer, TG can provide it in a concise and informative way.

- **Generating Summaries:** If the answer is more complex, TG can summarize the key points from the retrieved information.

- **Creative Text Formats (Exploratory):** While still under development, researchers are exploring using RAG for creative text formats like poems, code, or scripts based on the extracted information. Imagine providing keywords or a starting line, and RAG generates a creative text format inspired by those prompts and the information it finds.

Here's a (hypothetical) code snippet to illustrate how prompt engineering can influence response generation (remember, this is not real code):

Python

```python
def generate_response(prompt,
extracted_info):

  # Process the prompt to understand the
  task and desired style

  task = get_task_from_prompt(prompt)

                  style          =
  get_style_from_prompt(prompt)



    # Use the prompt, extracted
  information, task, and style to craft the
  response

  response = ""

  if task == "answer_question":
```

```
        response     =
answer_question(extracted_info)

  elif task == "summarize":

    response = summarize(extracted_info)

  # ... (code to handle other tasks)


  # Apply stylistic elements based on the
identified style

  response = apply_style(response, style)


  return response
```

This is a simplified example, of course. In reality, the inner workings of TG are much more complex. But hopefully, this gives you a basic understanding of how prompt engineering and response generation work within RAG.

In the next chapter, we'll move beyond the basics and explore some advanced RAG techniques that push the boundaries of information retrieval and text generation. Get ready for even more exciting capabilities of this groundbreaking technology!

Chapter 3: Mastering the Fundamentals of AI for RAG

Now that we've explored the core workflow of RAG, let's delve deeper into the underlying AI technologies that make it tick. Think of RAG as a powerful engine, and in this chapter, we'll unwrap the key components that drive that engine.

3.1 Understanding Large Language Models (LLMs) and their role in RAG

Remember the superstar in Chapter 2, the creative writer who took center stage in crafting informative responses? That's the role Large Language Models (LLMs) play within RAG. Think of them as AI whizzes with a knack for generating all sorts of creative text formats, from poems to code.

Here's how LLMs fuel the Text Generation (TG) engine of RAG:

- **Language Masters:** LLMs are trained on massive amounts of text data, like books, articles, and code. This data becomes their training ground, allowing them to grasp the intricacies of language, including grammar, syntax, and semantics.

This mastery is crucial for generating natural-sounding and coherent responses tailored to your needs.

- **Text Generation Powerhouse:** Imagine a toolbox overflowing with creative writing tools. That's essentially what LLMs offer to RAG. Based on the information provided, LLMs can generate different creative text formats. They can craft summaries of complex topics, answer your questions directly in a clear and concise way, or even attempt more artistic endeavors like writing poems (still under development for RAG).

Think of LLMs as the artist within RAG. The information retrieved by IR provides the raw materials - the colors, shapes, and ideas. LLMs use their language skills to paint a compelling and informative response, just like an artist transforming a blank canvas.

Here's a (hypothetical) code snippet to illustrate how an LLM might be used for text generation (remember, this is not real code):

Python

```python
def generate_text(prompt, context):

    # Process the prompt and context to
    understand the task and desired style
```

```
# ... (code to process prompt and
context)



# Leverage the LLM's capabilities based
on the processed information
        internal_representation      =
get_internal_representation(prompt,
context)

            generated_text      =
predict(internal_representation,  model)
# Model refers to the LLM



# Apply post-processing steps (optional)
to refine the generated text
```

```
# ... (code for post-processing)



return generated_text
```

This is a simplified example, of course. Real LLMs are much more complex, but hopefully, this gives you a basic idea of how they work within the RAG framework.

Beyond the code, it's important to remember that LLMs are still under development. As researchers continue to refine them, we can expect even more impressive capabilities in the future, opening doors for even richer and more creative text generation within RAG.

3.2 Introduction to Information Retrieval Techniques: Diving Deeper Than Keywords

Remember the super-powered librarian from Chapter 2, the one who tirelessly searched for the most relevant information for RAG? But how exactly does this librarian find the perfect documents? Here, we'll explore two key information retrieval (IR) techniques: keyword search and semantic similarity. Think of them as superpowers that help IR find the bullseye!

1. Keyword Search: The Classic Approach

Imagine searching for a book in a library by flipping through the card catalog and looking for a specific title match. That's essentially keyword search in action. IR scans documents for keywords present in your query. While this is a simple and straightforward approach, it has limitations:

- **Limited Scope:** Keyword search might miss relevant documents that don't contain the exact keywords you used, even if they discuss similar concepts.
- **Synonym Blindness:** If your query uses synonyms or related

terms not present in the documents, IR might overlook them altogether.

Here's an example:

- **Query:** "Best laptops for students on a budget"
- **Keyword Search (Limited):** IR might find documents mentioning "laptops" but not necessarily targetted towards students or budget-conscious buyers.

2. Semantic Similarity: Understanding the True Meaning

This is where things get interesting! IR goes beyond just keywords. Think of it as graduating from the card catalog to actually reading the book summaries. IR tries to understand the meaning behind the words and their relationships to each other. Imagine grasping the context of your query. This allows IR to find documents that discuss similar concepts even if they don't use the exact words you used.

Here's how semantic similarity empowers IR:

- **Identifying Synonyms and Related Concepts:** IR can recognize synonyms and related terms for the keywords in your query, broadening the search scope and potentially finding more relevant documents.

- **Understanding Context:** IR considers the context of your query and the context of the documents. This helps identify documents that might not have the exact keywords but still address your information needs.

Here's an example of how semantic similarity refines the search:

- **Query:** "Best laptops for students on a budget"
- **Semantic Similarity (Powerful):** IR can understand the context and find documents discussing affordable laptops suitable for student use, even if the

exact phrase "laptops for students on a budget" isn't used.

By combining keyword search with semantic similarity, IR becomes a more powerful tool for finding the most relevant information for RAG. Imagine searching a library with both the card catalog (keywords) and insightful summaries (semantic similarity) – that's the power of these combined techniques!

Code Example (Illustrative, Not Real Code):

Python

```python
def retrieve_information(query, documents):
```

```python
# Step 1: Keyword Matching (Basic
Search)

candidate_documents = []

for keyword in query.split():

    for document in documents:

        if keyword in document:


candidate_documents.append(document
)



# Step 2: Semantic Similarity (Advanced
Search)

    # (This part would likely involve
techniques like word embeddings)
```

```
# ... (code for semantic similarity
analysis)

# ... (filter candidate_documents based
on semantic similarity scores)



return relevant_documents
```

This is a simplified example, of course.
Real IR systems use much more
sophisticated techniques for semantic
similarity analysis. But hopefully, this
helps illustrate the concept and its power
in information retrieval for RAG.

3.3 Familiarizing Yourself with Transformers: The Powerhouse Behind RAG's Success

Remember the engine powering a car? That unseen force that makes everything move? Similarly, transformers play a crucial role in many RAG models. Think of them as a powerful and innovative neural network architecture specifically designed to excel at understanding relationships between words. They act like the engine processing information within RAG, allowing it to function at its best.

Here's why transformers are so important for RAG:

- **Efficient Text Processing Power:** Imagine a factory that can churn through massive amounts of raw materials quickly. That's what transformers bring to the table. They can process large amounts of text data efficiently, which is essential for training the LLMs (Large Language Models) used in RAG's text generation (TG) component. These LLMs require vast amounts of text data to learn the nuances of language and generate creative text formats.

- **Capturing Relationships Between Words:** Understanding how words connect and interact is fundamental to both understanding and generating human language. Here's where transformers shine. They are adept at capturing these relationships within sentences and across entire documents. This ability is crucial for several reasons:

- **Accurate Text Generation:** By understanding how words connect, LLMs within RAG can generate more coherent and grammatically correct text.

- **Semantic Search Enhancement:** Transformers can potentially be used to improve information retrieval (IR) by understanding the semantic relationships between the query and the documents in the collection. This can lead to finding more relevant information even if the exact keywords aren't used.

While the inner workings of transformers are quite complex, here's a simplified analogy to grasp their essence:

- Imagine a sentence as a train with multiple cars. Each car represents a word, and the connections between the cars represent the relationships between the words.

- A standard neural network might analyze each car (word) independently.
- Transformers, on the other hand, can analyze not only the individual cars (words) but also the connections between them (relationships). This allows them to understand the overall meaning of the sentence more effectively.

Code Example (Illustrative, Not Real Code):

Python

```
# This is a high-level representation, not actual code for a transformer.

def process_text(text):
```

```
# Tokenization: Break the text into
individual words (like splitting the train
into cars)

words = tokenize(text)


# Pass the words through the
transformer model

            encoded_text        =
transformer_encoder(words)


# The encoded text captures the
relationships between the words

return encoded_text
```

This is a very simplified example, of course. Real transformers are much more complex and involve intricate mathematical calculations. But hopefully, this gives you a basic understanding of how transformers work and why they are so valuable for RAG, especially when it comes to training LLMs and potentially enhancing IR.

As researchers continue to explore and refine transformers, we can expect them to play an even greater role in the future of RAG and other AI applications that rely on understanding and generating human language.

Chapter 4: Beyond the Basics: Advanced Retrieval Techniques for RAG

We've explored the core functionalities of RAG, but there's always room for improvement! This chapter dives into some advanced information retrieval (IR) techniques that push RAG's capabilities even further. Think of these techniques as special tools that help RAG find the most relevant and informative pieces of information to power its text generation.

4.1 Sentence-window Retrieval: Focusing on the Bullseye

Remember the treasure hunt from our childhood? We wouldn't just aimlessly search the entire park; we'd focus on specific areas marked on the treasure map. Sentence-window retrieval in RAG adopts a similar strategy for information retrieval (IR). Imagine it as a laser beam that zooms in on the exact bits of information you need, rather than returning entire documents that might be filled with irrelevant details.

Traditional Retrieval: Delivering the Whole Library

Think back to the days of paper libraries. When you asked a librarian a question, they might hand you a stack of books related to your topic. While helpful, this approach isn't the most efficient. You'd likely spend a lot of time sifting through irrelevant pages to find the specific answer you seek.

This is analogous to basic retrieval in RAG. IR scans documents for keywords present in your query and returns those documents. While it gets the job done, it can be cumbersome, especially for complex topics or when the answer might be buried within a lengthy document.

Sentence-window Retrieval: Sharpening the Focus

Sentence-window retrieval takes a more targeted approach. Instead of returning entire documents, IR hones in on the specific sentences within those documents that directly answer your question or provide the most relevant information. Imagine the librarian handing you not just the relevant books, but also highlighting the exact passages that address your query.

Here's an example to illustrate the difference:

- **Query:** "What is the capital of France?"
- **Traditional Retrieval:** IR might return various documents about France, including historical

documents or travel guides. You'd then need to scan through these documents to find the answer.

- **Sentence-window Retrieval (Improved):** IR narrows down the search and retrieves the specific sentence that states "Paris is the capital of France."

Benefits of Sentence-window Retrieval:

- **Improved Context:** By focusing on relevant sentences, RAG can grasp the surrounding context of the answer, leading to more informative responses that go beyond just providing factual statements.

- **Reduced Redundancy:** This technique avoids returning entire documents that might contain irrelevant information, streamlining the retrieval process and potentially reducing the amount of data RAG needs to process for text generation.

Here's a (hypothetical) code snippet to illustrate the concept (remember, this is not real code):

Python

```python
def retrieve_sentences(query, documents):
```

```
# Identify relevant documents using
traditional retrieval methods (not shown
here)

relevant_documents = ...


# Loop through each document and
identify relevant sentences

sentences = []

for document in relevant_documents:

    for sentence in document.split("."):

        if query_matches_sentence(query,
sentence):  # Replace with a function for
semantic matching

            sentences.append(sentence)
```

return sentences

This is a simplified example, of course. Real-world implementations might involve more sophisticated techniques for identifying relevant sentences based on semantic similarity and other factors, like the position of the sentence within a document or its proximity to other relevant keywords.

4.2 Hybrid Search: The Best of Both Worlds

Imagine searching for information online. Sometimes you might use very specific keywords, like searching for "car maintenance manual for a 2020 Honda Civic." Other times, you might use broader search terms, like "tips for keeping my car in good shape." RAG's hybrid search takes a page out of your search strategy, combining the strengths of different information retrieval (IR) techniques for optimal results.

Think of it like having two powerful search tools in your RAG toolbox:

- **Keyword Search: The Tried-and-True Method:** This is the workhorse of traditional search. IR scans documents for the exact keywords present in your query. It's straightforward and efficient for queries with clear keywords.

- **Semantic Search: Understanding the Deeper Meaning:** This goes beyond just keywords. Semantic search tries to grasp the meaning behind the words and their relationships. Think of it like trying to understand the intent behind your query. This allows IR to find documents that discuss similar concepts even if they don't use the exact words you used.

Hybrid Search: Combining Forces for Better Results

Hybrid search in RAG brings these two techniques together, leveraging the strengths of each:

- **Flexibility:** Hybrid search can adapt to different query styles. For exact-match queries, keyword search can take center stage. For broader queries where you're exploring a topic, semantic search can play a more prominent role, complementing the keyword search and potentially uncovering unexpectedly relevant information.

- **Improved Accuracy:** By combining keyword matching with semantic similarity, hybrid search can potentially reduce the chances of missing relevant information due to over-reliance on exact keywords alone. Imagine searching for "fuel-efficient cars" – hybrid search might not only find documents mentioning those exact words but also uncover documents discussing "eco-friendly vehicles" or "cars with good gas mileage," expanding the scope of relevant information retrieved.

Here's a conceptual code example (illustrative, not real code) to show the essence of hybrid search:

Python

```python
def hybrid_search(query, documents):
```

```
# Perform keyword search and semantic
search independently (not shown here)

keyword_results = ...

semantic_results = ...


# Combine the results using appropriate
weighting factors

        combined_results        =
merge_results(keyword_results,
semantic_results)

return combined_results
```

This is a high-level representation, of
course. Real-world implementations

might involve more intricate methods for combining and ranking search results. For instance, documents retrieved through keyword search might be given higher weight compared to those found through semantic search, depending on the specificity of the query.

The key takeaway is that hybrid search allows RAG to cast a wider net while still focusing on relevant information, ultimately leading to more comprehensive and informative responses.

4.3   Auto-merging   Retrieval: Creating a Cohesive Narrative

Imagine you're a detective putting together a case. You wouldn't just throw all the random clues in a pile and expect to solve the mystery, right? You'd meticulously analyze each piece of evidence, understand how they connect, and create a coherent narrative. Auto-merging retrieval in RAG follows a similar approach, aiming to weave together the retrieved information to create a seamless response.

Traditional Retrieval: Delivering Raw Materials

Think back to how basic information retrieval (IR) works in RAG. It acts like a research assistant who finds a bunch of documents related to your query. These documents might be relevant, but they're presented as separate entities, like a pile of unorganized research papers.

This can be cumbersome for RAG's Text Generation (TG) component. While TG can process this information, it requires additional effort to extract the key points, understand the relationships between the retrieved documents, and synthesize them into a cohesive response that addresses your query.

Auto-merging Retrieval: Building a Story

Auto-merging retrieval goes beyond just delivering the raw materials. It acts like a sophisticated research assistant who not only finds relevant documents but also analyzes them, identifies the key points, and merges the information into a coherent summary or narrative tailored to your query.

Here's how auto-merging retrieval enhances the process:

- **Structured Information:** It transforms the retrieved documents from a scattered collection into a structured format, highlighting the essential information relevant to the query.

- **Context Integration:** Auto-merging retrieval considers the context of your query and tailors the information accordingly.

Imagine the research assistant summarizing the key points while keeping your question in mind.

- **Improved Cohesion:** By merging the information seamlessly, auto-merging retrieval helps TG generate more cohesive and informative responses that flow naturally.

Here's a conceptual code example (illustrative, not real code) to give you a basic idea:

Python

```python
def auto_merge_retrieval(query, documents):
```

```
# Retrieve documents using traditional
methods (not shown here)

retrieved_documents = ...


# Analyze and extract key information
from each document

extracted_info = []
for document in retrieved_documents:


extracted_info.append(summarize_key_
points(document, query))


# Merge the information based on
relevance and query context
```

```
        merged_information        =
combine_and_summarize(extracted_inf
o, query)


    return merged_information
```

This is a simplified example, of course. Real-world implementations might involve more advanced techniques for information extraction, summarization, and merging, potentially using natural language processing (NLP) approaches.

The key takeaway is that auto-merging retrieval plays a crucial role in transforming disparate pieces of information

into a cohesive narrative, ultimately empowering RAG to deliver high-quality and informative responses.

Chapter 5: Fine-Tuning the Generation Process: Sculpting the Art of Response Crafting

We've explored the core functionalities of RAG, but just like a sculptor refines a block of clay, we can further enhance RAG's text generation (TG) capabilities. This chapter dives into techniques for crafting the perfect prompt, a crucial element that guides RAG's LLM (Large Language Model) towards generating the desired response.

5.1 Crafting Effective Prompts for RAG: The Art of the Perfect Prompt

Imagine you're instructing a master chef to create a delicious dish. A simple "make me something to eat" wouldn't quite cut it, right? You'd provide specific details about your preferences. Similarly, crafting effective prompts for RAG's Large Language Model (LLM) is essential for guiding it towards generating the desired response. Think of the prompt as a detailed recipe for the LLM, instructing it on exactly what kind of textual dish to cook up for you.

Here are the key ingredients for an effective RAG prompt:

- **Clarity and Specificity:** Avoid vague instructions. Be clear about the topic you want the LLM to address and the type of response you desire. For instance, a prompt for summarizing a scientific article would differ from a prompt for writing a funny poem.

- **Context is King:** Provide relevant background information to the LLM. This could include details related to your query, previous interactions with RAG, or any specific requirements you have. The more context you provide, the better the LLM can understand the bigger picture and tailor its response accordingly.

- **Desired Tone and Style:** Let the LLM know the flavor you're looking for in the generated text. Do you want a formal analysis, a casual conversation, or something creative and whimsical? Specifying the tone and style helps the LLM season the response with the right characteristics.

Here's an example to illustrate the difference between a vague and an effective prompt:

- **Vague Prompt:** "Tell me about animals." (This prompt is too broad and doesn't provide any direction.)
- **Effective Prompt:** "Summarize a factual article about the impact of climate change on endangered animal species. Highlight the specific challenges different animals face and mention any conservation efforts underway." (This prompt is clear, informative, and specifies the desired style - a factual summary.)

Code Example (Illustrative):

Python

```python
def generate_text(prompt, context):
```

```
# Process the prompt to understand the
task, desired style, and context (not
shown here)

processed_prompt = ...


# Leverage the LLM based on the
processed prompt and context

generated_text =
predict(processed_prompt, model) #
Model refers to the LLM


return generated_text
```

This is a simplified example, of course. In reality, prompt processing might involve techniques like information extraction and Natural Language Processing (NLP) to enrich the prompt with the necessary details for the LLM to understand your request fully.

By following these tips and using clear, informative prompts, you can become a master chef in the kitchen of RAG, instructing the LLM to generate well-crafted and informative responses that hit the spot every time.

5.2 Exploring Advanced Prompt Engineering Techniques:

Conditioning and Temperature Control

Crafting effective prompts is a foundational skill for coaxing the best responses from RAG's Large Language Model (LLM). But RAG offers even more tools in its toolbox! Imagine these as dials and levers you can adjust to fine-tune the generation process for even more impressive results. Here, we'll delve into two such techniques: conditioning and temperature control.

1. Conditioning: Guiding the LLM with Specificity

Think of conditioning as a way to provide additional instructions or information within the prompt itself. Imagine whispering specific directions to the LLM while it cooks up your textual dish. This extra guidance helps steer the LLM in a particular direction, influencing the content and style of the generated text.

Here's an example of how conditioning can be used:

- **Prompt (without conditioning):** "Write a poem about nature." (This prompt is quite open-ended.)
- **Prompt (with conditioning):** "Write a poem about nature. Focus on themes of tranquility and renewal. Use vivid imagery to paint a picture of a peaceful forest at

dawn." (This conditioned prompt provides specific instructions regarding the desired mood, style, and even imagery.)

By incorporating conditioning information, you can nudge the LLM to generate text that aligns more closely with your specific requirements.

2. Temperature Control: Balancing Creativity with Accuracy

Imagine a temperature dial on a kitchen stove. Similarly, temperature control in RAG allows you to adjust the randomness of the generated text. This can be a powerful tool for achieving the desired balance between creativity and factuality.

- **High Temperature (More Creative):** Think of this as setting the stove to high heat. The LLM will explore a wider range of possibilities, potentially generating more creative and original text formats. However, there's an increased chance of the LLM straying from factual accuracy or introducing irrelevant information.

- **Low Temperature (More Factual):** This is like simmering your creation on low heat. The LLM will focus on generating safe, predictable text that adheres closely to the provided information and context. While this can be beneficial for ensuring factual accuracy, it might also lead to less imaginative or interesting responses.

Here's an analogy to illustrate temperature control:

- **High Temperature:** Brainstorming many creative ideas without worrying too much about feasibility - like throwing random ingredients into a pot and hoping for the best.

- **Low Temperature:** Carefully considering every detail to ensure a predictable outcome - like following a recipe to the letter.

Code Example (Illustrative):

Python

```python
def generate_text(prompt, conditioning_info, temperature):

  # Process the prompt, conditioning info, and temperature (not shown here)

  processed_info = ...


  # Leverage the LLM based on the processed information

  generated_text = predict(processed_info, model)
```

```
return generated_text
```

Remember, this is a simplified example. Real-world implementations might involve more sophisticated techniques for incorporating conditioning information and temperature control.

By using conditioning and temperature control effectively, you can become a master chef in the RAG kitchen. Conditioning provides specific instructions, while temperature control allows you to fine-tune the level of creativity and risk tolerance. Experimenting with these techniques will help you craft the perfect recipe for generating high-quality and informative responses from RAG's LLM.

5.3 Controlling Factual Accuracy and Avoiding Hallucinations in Generated Text: Keeping RAG Grounded in Reality

RAG's ability to generate creative text formats is like having a powerful storytelling machine at your fingertips. But just like a campfire story might contain fantastical elements, RAG's Large Language Model (LLM) can sometimes veer off course, unintentionally generating inaccurate information or straying into the realm of "hallucinations" – fabricated details that weren't present in the factual data it was trained on. Here, we'll explore techniques to ensure RAG's responses stay rooted in reality.

Understanding Hallucinations in RAG:

Imagine a child excitedly recounting a dream. Their story might be vivid and engaging, but it might also contain fantastical elements that didn't actually happen. Similarly, RAG's LLM, despite being trained on massive amounts of data, can sometimes weave fictional details into its generated text.

Here are some reasons why hallucinations might occur:

Limited Context: If the prompt or retrieved information lacks sufficient context, the LLM might make assumptions or fill in the gaps with its own creative interpretations.

Statistical Biases: The training data itself might contain biases or inaccuracies, which the LLM can unintentionally inherit and perpetuate in its generated text.

Techniques to Mitigate Hallucinations:

- **Fact-checking and Grounding:** Just like double-checking a recipe before baking a cake, you can leverage RAG's information retrieval (IR) capabilities to verify the factual accuracy of the generated text against reliable sources. This helps ground the response in reality.

Here's a conceptual code example (illustrative):

Python

```python
def generate_text(prompt, context):

    # Generate text using LLM (not shown here)
```

```
generated_text = ...
```

```
# Fact-check the generated text using retrieved information (not shown here)
```

```
fact_checked_text = verify_factuality(generated_text, retrieved_info)
```

```
return fact_checked_text
```

- **Improving Prompt Quality:** As discussed earlier, crafting clear and informative prompts is crucial. Precise prompts that specify the desired factual accuracy level can help guide the LLM towards generating more reliable text.

- **Leveraging External Knowledge Sources:** RAG can integrate with external knowledge bases or fact-checking APIs to access real-time information and verify the factuality of its outputs during the generation process.

It's important to remember that RAG is still under development, and continual research is being conducted to improve factual grounding. However, by using the techniques mentioned above, you can significantly reduce the risk of hallucinations and ensure RAG's responses are grounded in factual accuracy.

The key takeaway is to be aware of the potential for hallucinations and implement safeguards to maintain the reliability of RAG's generated text. By combining RAG's creative capabilities with a focus on factual accuracy, you can unlock its full potential as a powerful information and storytelling tool.

Chapter 6: Evaluating RAG Performance

So, you've been whipping up delicious dishes (text responses) with RAG, but how do you know they're truly satisfying? Just like any good chef monitors their creations, evaluating RAG's performance is essential. This chapter dives into various metrics to assess RAG's effectiveness, ensuring it delivers high-quality, informative, and unbiased responses.

6.1 Understanding Different Metrics for Measuring RAG Effectiveness: Picking the Right Tools for the Job

Imagine you're a food critic evaluating dishes in a competition. You wouldn't rely solely on taste, would you? You'd consider presentation, portion size, creativity, and adherence to the recipe. Similarly, effectively evaluating RAG's performance requires a multi-faceted approach using various metrics. Think of these metrics as your evaluation tools, each providing a different perspective on how well RAG is performing its text-chef duties.

Here are some key metrics to consider,
along with what they tell you about
RAG's outputs:

- **Relevance:** This metric cuts to the
  heart of whether RAG hits the
  bullseye. Does the generated text
  directly address the user's query
  and provide information pertinent
  to their needs? Imagine a user
  asking for a recipe for chocolate
  chip cookies and receiving a lecture
  on the history of chocolate. That
  wouldn't be very relevant! Metrics
  like ROUGE score (measures
  overlap between generated text and
  reference summaries) can be used
  to assess relevance.

Here's a (simplified) code example to illustrate how ROUGE score might be calculated:

Python

```
def calculate_rouge(generated_text, reference_summary):

    # Split the text into bigrams and trigrams (sequences of words)

    generated_ngrams = extract_ngrams(generated_text, n=2, n=3)  # Bigrams and trigrams

    reference_ngrams = extract_ngrams(reference_summary, n=2, n=3)
```

```
    # Count the overlap between generated
and reference n-grams

        overlap_count          =
count_matches(generated_ngrams,
reference_ngrams)


    # Calculate ROUGE score based on
overlap and total n-grams in the
reference summary

    rouge_score = overlap_count /
total_ngrams(reference_summary, n=2,
n=3)


    return rouge_score
```

Remember, this is a simplified example. Real-world implementations might involve more sophisticated techniques for n-gram extraction and overlap counting.

- **Fluency and Coherence:** This metric looks at the language itself. Is the generated text grammatically correct, easy to read, and logically structured? Imagine a recipe with instructions that jump from step 5 to step 12! That would be confusing and hard to follow. Metrics like BLEU score (measures similarity between generated text and reference sentences) can be helpful for evaluation.

- **Informativeness:** This metric goes beyond just factual accuracy. Does the generated text provide valuable insights and comprehensive answers? Think of a recipe that simply says "bake for 20 minutes." While factually accurate, it doesn't provide much helpful information for a novice baker. Human evaluation remains an important tool for assessing the overall informativeness of the response, considering factors like the depth of explanation and inclusion of relevant details.

Choosing the right metrics depends on the specific task and your priorities. For example, if summarizing factual topics is the goal, relevance and ROUGE score become particularly important. If, however, you're evaluating a creative story generated by RAG, fluency and coherence might be more critical.

6.2 Evaluating Relevance, Groundedness, and Factual Accuracy: The Holy Trinity of Text Quality

Remember the old adage, "garbage in, garbage out"? It applies to RAG as well.

While RAG can be a powerful tool for generating text, the quality of its outputs hinges on three key factors: relevance, groundedness, and factual accuracy. Think of these three aspects as the holy trinity of text quality, working together to ensure RAG delivers informative and trustworthy responses.

- **Relevance: Staying on Target**

Imagine a customer asking a waiter for a recommendation and receiving a detailed explanation of the wine list. While the information might be interesting, it's not exactly relevant to the customer's immediate query. Similarly, relevance in RAG focuses on whether the generated text directly addresses the user's intention and provides information pertinent to their needs.

Here are some ways to evaluate relevance:

- Human evaluation: Read the generated text and ask yourself, "Does this answer the user's question in a clear and concise way?"
- Task-specific metrics: Depending on the task, metrics like ROUGE score (for summarization tasks) or click-through rates (for retrieval tasks) can be used to measure how well the generated text aligns with the user's intent.

- **Groundedness: Keeping it Real**

Think of a recipe that calls for a magical ingredient not found in any supermarket. That recipe might sound fantastical, but it's not very grounded in reality. Groundedness in RAG refers to how well the generated text is supported by factual evidence and avoids straying into the realm of fantasy or unsubstantiated claims.

Here are some ways to evaluate groundedness:

- Fact-checking: Use external knowledge sources or fact-checking APIs to verify the factual accuracy of the claims made in the generated text.

- Consistency with retrieved information: If RAG retrieves documents during the generation process, ensure the generated text aligns with the factual content of those documents.

- **Factual Accuracy: Building Trust**

Just like a recipe needs the correct measurements to produce a delicious dish, RAG's responses need to be factually accurate to be truly valuable. Imagine a recipe that incorrectly states the baking temperature for cookies. Following those instructions could lead to burnt cookies and a disappointed baker! Factual accuracy ensures the information presented in the generated text is reliable and trustworthy.

Here are some ways to evaluate factual accuracy:

- Fact-checking against credible sources: Verify the information in the generated text against established knowledge bases or reliable websites.
- Human evaluation with domain expertise: Involve subject-matter experts to evaluate the factual accuracy of the generated text, particularly for complex topics.

The interplay between these three metrics is crucial. Highly relevant text might not be factually accurate, and grounded text might lack informativeness. By evaluating all three aspects, you can ensure RAG generates high-quality responses that hit the mark for relevance, stay grounded in reality, and provide trustworthy information.

6.3 Analyzing Bias and Fairness in Retrieved Information and Generated Text: Keeping RAG Unbiased

Imagine a cookbook filled only with recipes from one specific culture. That wouldn't be a very fair or inclusive representation of the culinary world, right? Similarly, when evaluating RAG's performance, it's important to consider potential biases and fairness issues in both the information it retrieves and the text it generates.

- **Bias in Retrieved Information:**
  - RAG relies on massive datasets of text and code for training. These datasets themselves might contain inherent biases that can influence the information RAG retrieves. For instance, if a training dataset primarily consists of news articles from

a specific region, the retrieved information might reflect the perspectives and biases prevalent in that region.

- **Bias in Generated Text:**
  - The way RAG processes information and generates text can also introduce bias. Here's how:
    - **Algorithmic Bias:** Biases in the underlying algorithms used by RAG can creep into the generated text. For example, if an algorithm is better at recognizing and associating certain

words with particular genders, the generated text might perpetuate those stereotypes.

- **Data Bias:** Biases within the training data can be reflected in the generated text. If the training data primarily features examples of one demographic group in a particular profession, RAG might be more likely to generate text that reinforces that association.

Here's how to mitigate bias in RAG:

- **Using Diverse Training Datasets:** By incorporating a wider variety of sources from different cultures, viewpoints, and backgrounds into the training data, bias can be reduced.

- **Debiasing Techniques During Text Generation:** Techniques like fairness aware algorithms can be implemented during text generation to minimize the influence of biases in the underlying algorithms. These algorithms might involve adjusting the language model's output to promote fairer representations across different groups.

Here's a conceptual code example (illustrative) to give you a basic idea of fairness-aware algorithms:

Python

```
def generate_text(prompt, context,
fairness_constraints):

  # Process the prompt, context, and
  fairness constraints (not shown
  here)

  processed_info = ...


  # Leverage the LLM with bias
  mitigation techniques (not shown
  here)
```

```
        generated_text        =
fair_generate(processed_info,
model)


return generated_text
```

This is a simplified example, of course.
Real-world implementations of
fairness-aware algorithms might involve
complex techniques like modifying the
model's loss function or incorporating
fairness metrics into the generation
process.

Evaluating Fairness:

- **Fairness Scores:** Metrics like demographic parity scores can be used to assess whether different groups are represented fairly in the generated text. For instance, a fair response about occupations shouldn't favor one gender over another in its wording or examples.
- **Human Evaluation:** Ultimately, human evaluation remains crucial for identifying and mitigating bias in RAG's outputs. People can assess whether the generated text presents a balanced and inclusive perspective.

By continuously evaluating and mitigating bias, you can ensure

RAG generates fair and trustworthy text that represents the world in all its diversity.

Chapter 7: Building Your Own RAG Pipeline: Cooking Up Text with RAG in Python

So far, we've explored the magic behind RAG. Now, let's get our hands dirty and build our very own RAG pipeline! This chapter dives into the practicalities of implementing RAG using Python, focusing on essential tools, data preparation, and fine-tuning for specific tasks.

7.1 Choosing the Right Tools and Libraries for RAG Implementation (Python Focus)

Building your own RAG pipeline is like assembling a top-notch kitchen! Just like different recipes require specific tools, the libraries you choose for your RAG implementation will depend on the complexity of your project. Here, we'll focus on the essential Python libraries that act as your key ingredients for cooking up delicious text with RAG.

The Core Library: Transformers

Imagine having a well-stocked pantry filled with all the essentials. The Transformers library is like that pantry for your RAG project. It provides the foundation upon which everything else rests. Here's what Transformers offers:

- **Pre-trained RAG Models:** You don't have to start from scratch! Transformers provides access to a variety of pre-trained RAG models, like facebook/bart-base-model, already trained on massive amounts of text data. These models can be fine-tuned for your specific needs (more on that later).
- **Tokenization Power:** Just like chopping vegetables is a crucial first step in many recipes, tokenization is essential for text processing in RAG. Transformers provides

tokenizers that break down text into smaller units (tokens) that the model can understand.

- **Text Processing Techniques:** Transformers offers functionalities for various text processing tasks, including encoding text for model input and decoding model outputs back into human-readable text.

Here's a code snippet (illustrative) showcasing how you might load a pre-trained RAG model and tokenizer from Transformers:

Python

```python
from transformers import
AutoModelForSeq2SeqLM,
AutoTokenizer


# Select a pre-trained RAG model
(example)
model_name =
"facebook/bart-base-model"


# Load the model and tokenizer
model =
AutoModelForSeq2SeqLM.from_pretrai
ned(model_name)
```

```
tokenizer                          =
AutoTokenizer.from_pretrained(model_
name)
```

Beyond the Core: Additional Libraries for Specific Needs

While Transformers provides the core functionalities, you might need additional libraries depending on your project's complexity:

- **Datasets:** Libraries like Hugging Face Datasets offer a treasure trove of pre-processed datasets you can leverage for training or fine-tuning your RAG model. These datasets can save you significant time and effort compared to preparing data from scratch.

- **Information Retrieval (IR) Libraries:** If your RAG project involves retrieving relevant information from large document stores, then IR libraries like Faiss or haystack become essential ingredients. These libraries help RAG efficiently find the information it needs to inform its text generation.

- **Evaluation Libraries:** Once you've built your RAG pipeline, you'll want to evaluate its performance. Libraries like Rouge or SacreBLEU provide metrics like

BLEU score (measures similarity between generated text and reference sentences) to assess how well your RAG model is performing.

Choosing the right libraries boils down to understanding your project's specific requirements. For a simple task like text summarization using a pre-trained model, you might just need Transformers. For a more complex project involving information retrieval and custom evaluation metrics, you might need the entire toolkit!

7.2 Data Preparation and Pre-processing for Optimal RAG Performance

Imagine a chef receiving a messy bag of vegetables for a delicate dish. They wouldn't jump straight to cooking, right? They'd meticulously clean and prepare the ingredients to ensure the final dish is perfect. Similarly, data preparation and pre-processing are crucial steps for optimal RAG performance. Think of it as getting your ingredients – your text data – ready for RAG to cook up informative and accurate responses.

Here are the key steps involved in data preparation and pre-processing for RAG:

- **Data Cleaning:** Just like washing and trimming vegetables, data cleaning involves removing any impurities from your text data. This includes:
  - **Error Correction:** Fixing typos, grammatical mistakes, and inconsistencies in your data. Imagine using a recipe riddled with typos – it could lead to disastrous results!
  - **Normalization:** Converting all text to lowercase or uppercase for consistency. Think of chopping all your vegetables into uniform pieces for even cooking.

- **Noise Removal:** Removing irrelevant symbols, punctuation (except for specific cases), and special characters that might confuse the model. Imagine finding a toy car in your vegetable bag – it doesn't belong there!

- **Data Pre-processing:** This is where you transform your cleaned data into a format understandable by the RAG model. Here's what pre-processing might involve:

  - **Tokenization:** Breaking down your text into smaller units (tokens) – words, subwords, or characters – that the model can process. Think of chopping vegetables into bite-sized pieces for easier handling.

- ○ **Building Vocabulary:** Creating a dictionary that maps each unique token to a numerical representation. This allows the model to efficiently understand and manipulate the text. Imagine labeling each ingredient in your kitchen with a code for easy identification.

- ○ **Text Encoding:** Converting the tokenized text into numerical sequences that the model can use for calculations. Think of a recipe using numbers to indicate quantities – 2 cups of flour, 1 teaspoon of salt.

Here's a code snippet (illustrative) to show basic tokenization using Transformers:

Python

```python
from transformers import AutoTokenizer

# Sample text

text = "This is a sample sentence for tokenization."
```

```
# Load a tokenizer (assuming you
already have a pre-trained model loaded)

tokenizer = model.get_tokenizer()  # Get
tokenizer from the loaded model


# Tokenize the text

tokens = tokenizer.tokenize(text)


print(tokens)   # Output: ['This', 'is', 'a',
'sample', 'sentence', 'for', 'tokenization',
'.']
```

The level of data pre-processing required depends on the format of your data and the specific needs of your RAG task. For example, if your data is already clean and well-structured, you might not need extensive cleaning. However, if your data is messy or contains specific domain-related jargon, you might need additional pre-processing steps.

Remember, high-quality data preparation is an investment that pays off in the long run. Clean and well-preprocessed data leads to a better understanding for the RAG model, resulting in more accurate and informative text generation.

7.3 Fine-tuning Pre-trained Models for Specific Tasks and Domains: Specializing Your RAG Chef

Imagine a world-class chef who excels at French cuisine but needs to create an authentic Thai dish. They wouldn't throw away all their skills and knowledge, would they? Instead, they'd leverage their expertise while adapting their techniques to the specific ingredients and flavors of Thai cooking. Similarly, fine-tuning a pre-trained RAG model allows you to specialize it for a particular task or domain.

Why Fine-tune? The Power of Adaptation

Pre-trained RAG models are like culinary masters with a vast knowledge base. They've been trained on massive amounts of text data, giving them a strong foundation for understanding language. However, just like a chef wouldn't use the same recipe for every dish, you might want to fine-tune a pre-trained RAG model for your specific needs. Here's why fine-tuning is beneficial:

- **Improved Performance:** Fine-tuning allows the model to focus on the particularities of your task or domain. Imagine a pre-trained RAG model excelling at summarizing general news articles. Fine-tuning it for summarizing medical research papers would significantly improve its performance in that specific domain by allowing it to learn the nuances of medical terminology and scientific writing style.

- **Reduced Training Time:** Fine-tuning leverages the pre-trained model's existing knowledge as a starting point. This is significantly faster and more efficient than training a model from scratch, especially for complex tasks. Think of it like the chef using their existing culinary skills as a foundation for learning a new cuisine.

How Fine-tuning Works: Adjusting the Recipe

Fine-tuning involves adjusting the weights of the pre-trained model based on your new training data specific to your task or domain. Here's a simplified analogy:

- Imagine the pre-trained model's weights as dials controlling its understanding of language. Fine-tuning involves slightly adjusting these dials based on your specific data. For example, a dial for recognizing medical terms might be increased in importance during fine-tuning for the medical domain.

Here's a conceptual code example (illustrative) to give you a basic idea of fine-tuning:

Python

```
from transformers import Trainer



# Define your fine-tuning
parameters and training data (not
shown here)

training_args = ...

train_dataset = ...
```

```
# Create a Trainer object for
fine-tuning

trainer = Trainer(

    model=model,  # Pre-trained
RAG model

  args=training_args,

  train_dataset=train_dataset

)


# Fine-tune the model

trainer.train()
```

This is a simplified example, of course. Real-world implementations of fine-tuning might involve techniques like gradient descent to precisely adjust the model's weights based on the training data.

Fine-tuning is a powerful tool for unlocking the full potential of RAG for specific tasks and domains. By leveraging the pre-trained model's knowledge and adapting it to your needs, you can create a RAG model that's a true specialist in your domain, generating informative and accurate text responses.

Chapter 8: Advanced RAG Applications: Unleashing the Potential of Your Text Chef

We've explored the fundamentals of building and evaluating a RAG pipeline. Now, let's delve into the exciting world of advanced applications! This chapter showcases how RAG can be your culinary companion for various tasks, from answering questions with pinpoint accuracy to crafting captivating stories.

8.1 Utilizing RAG for Question Answering Systems with Improved Accuracy: The Super-powered FAQ Assistant

Ever feel like you're wading through an endless FAQ trying to find a specific answer? Imagine an intelligent system that can not only understand your question but also confidently deliver the answer you seek. That's the potential of RAG in question answering (QA) systems! By leveraging RAG's strengths, you can build super-powered FAQ assistants that provide users with pinpoint accuracy and insightful responses.

Here's how RAG takes your QA system to the next level:

- **Going Beyond Simple Keyword Matching:** Traditional QA systems often rely on keyword matching, which can lead to inaccurate answers if the user's question isn't phrased exactly like something in the database. RAG, on the other hand, understands the nuances of language. It can grasp the intent behind a question and analyze relevant information to generate a comprehensive response, even for open ended questions.

- **Think of it this way:** Imagine a user asks, "What caused the decline of the Roman Empire?" A keyword-based system might find documents mentioning the fall of Rome but might miss the mark on specific causes. RAG, however, can analyze documents about Roman history, political structures, and economic factors, identifying key themes and generating a response that explores the multifaceted reasons behind the empire's decline.

- **Accuracy Powered by Factual Grounding:** RAG doesn't just provide any answer; it strives for factual accuracy. By retrieving relevant documents and grounding its responses in evidence, RAG ensures the information it delivers is trustworthy and reliable. This is especially crucial for critical domains like healthcare or finance.

Here's a conceptual code example (illustrative) to show a simplified question-answering pipeline with RAG:

Python

```python
def answer_question(question, retriever, model):

    """
```

This function takes a user question, retrieves relevant documents using a retriever, and generates an answer using the RAG model.

Args:

question: The user's question as a string.

retriever: An information retrieval system that retrieves documents

based on the question.

model: The RAG model used to generate the answer.

Returns:

A string containing the answer to the user's question.

"""

Retrieve relevant documents using the retriever

```
retrieved_docs = retriever.retrieve(question)
```


Process the question and retrieved documents for the RAG model (not shown here)

```
processed_info = ...
```

```
# Generate the answer using the
processed information

        answer            =
model.generate(**processed_info)


    return answer
```

This is a simplified example, of course. Real-world implementations might involve sophisticated information retrieval techniques like Faiss or haystack, and more complex model architectures for improved answer generation.

By incorporating RAG into your QA system, you can empower users to get the information they need quickly and accurately, turning your FAQ into a true knowledge hub.

8.2 Leveraging RAG for Chatbot Development with Enhanced Information Retrieval: The Conversational Connoisseur

Imagine a world where chatbots aren't just pre-programmed responses on a loop, but engaging conversational partners that can truly understand your needs. That's the future of chatbots with RAG! By integrating RAG's information retrieval and text generation capabilities, you can create chatbots that are more like conversational connoisseurs, providing informative and relevant responses to user queries.

Here's how RAG elevates your chatbot game:

- **Understanding the Context:** RAG isn't just a one-question-at-a-time wonder. It can analyze the entire conversation history, understanding the context of the current query. Think of a user asking about restaurants after mentioning they're looking for Italian cuisine. A traditional chatbot might offer generic recommendations. A RAG-powered chatbot, however, can leverage the context to suggest Italian restaurants in the user's area, creating a more natural and user-friendly experience.

- **The Power of Contextual Information Retrieval:** With RAG, information retrieval goes beyond simple keyword matching. It can consider the context of the conversation to retrieve the most relevant information. Imagine a user asking "What are the opening hours?" after mentioning a specific museum earlier in the conversation. RAG can retrieve the museum's website or relevant database entry to provide the exact opening hours, not just generic information about opening hours in general.

- **Generating Informative Responses:** RAG's text-generation abilities go beyond simple "yes" or "no" answers. It can process retrieved information and generate well-structured and informative responses tailored to the conversation's flow. Think of a user asking about a complex topic like climate change. A RAG-powered chatbot can not only provide relevant information but can also structure its response in a way that's easy for the user to understand.

Here's a conceptual code example (illustrative) to show a simplified chatbot interaction with RAG:

Python

```python
def chatbot_response(user_message, conversation_history, retriever, model):
    """
```

This function takes a user message, considers the conversation history,

retrieves relevant information using a retriever, and generates a response

using the RAG model.

Args:

user_message: The user's current message as a string.

conversation_history: A list of previous messages in the conversation.

retriever: An information retrieval system that retrieves documents

based on the conversation context.

model: The RAG model used to generate the response.

Returns:

A string containing the chatbot's response to the user's message.

"""

```
    # Process the user message and
conversation history (not shown here)

    processed_context = ...


    # Retrieve relevant information using
the retriever

    retrieved_info =
retriever.retrieve(processed_context)
```

```
# Generate the response using the
processed context and retrieved
information

        response        =
model.generate(**processed_context,
retrieved_info)


    return response
```

This is a simplified example, of course. Real-world implementations might involve integrating RAG with dialogue management systems to handle complex conversation flows and ensure a smooth user experience.

By leveraging RAG's capabilities, you can create chatbots that are not just informative but also engaging, making them valuable tools for customer service, education, and various other applications.

8.3 Exploring the Potential of RAG for Creative Text Generation Tasks Like Story Writing: The Narrative Chef

So far, we've explored RAG's prowess in factual tasks. But what about its creative potential? Buckle up, because we're venturing into the exciting world of using RAG for creative text generation tasks, like story writing! Here, RAG transforms into a **narrative chef**, assisting writers with brainstorming ideas and exploring new narrative avenues.

Tapping into RAG's Creative Spark:

- **Storytelling with a Twist:** Imagine providing RAG with a starting sentence or a brief narrative prompt. RAG can then use its language processing abilities to weave a story around it. Think of it as a brainstorming partner, suggesting interesting plot twists, character development ideas, or unexpected turns of events. While still under development, RAG has the potential to be a valuable tool for writers experiencing creative block or seeking fresh inspiration.

- **Genre Exploration and Style Mimicking:** RAG can be fine-tuned on specific writing styles or genres. This opens doors to exciting possibilities. Imagine a horror writer feeding RAG classic horror stories and then prompting it to continue the narrative in the same eerie style. Or a sci-fi writer using RAG to explore different technological advancements within their fictional universe.

- **Beyond Stories: A Universe of Creative Text Formats:** The possibilities extend beyond stories.

RAG could be fine-tuned to generate poems that mimic the style of a particular poet, scripts adhering to specific formatting guidelines, or even song lyrics that capture a certain mood or theme.

Here are some important considerations to keep in mind:

- **Guiding the Narrative Chef:** While RAG can be a creative spark, it currently lacks the deep understanding of human emotions and experiences that human writers possess. Therefore, providing clear prompts and guidance is crucial to steer the narrative in the desired direction.

- **Human-in-the-Loop Approach:** Think of RAG as a collaborator, not a replacement for human creativity. The best results might come from a combination of human imagination and RAG's ability to process information and generate creative text formats.

Overall, exploring RAG's creative potential is an ongoing adventure. As RAG develops further, it has the potential to become a powerful tool for writers and creatives, aiding them in their endeavors and

pushing the boundaries of imaginative expression.

Chapter 9: The Future of RAG

We've delved into the exciting world of RAG, exploring its capabilities and applications. But RAG is a continuously evolving field, with researchers constantly pushing the boundaries. In this chapter, we'll peek into the crystal ball and explore some emerging trends and advancements shaping the future of RAG.

9.1 Exploring Ongoing Research in RAG: Demystifying the Black Box

RAG models are powerful tools, but like any complex system, their inner workings can be a mystery. This lack of transparency can be a hurdle for trust and wider adoption. Researchers are actively working on ways to make RAG models more **explainable** and **interpretable**. Let's delve into what these terms mean and how they're being explored in the context of RAG.

Why Explainability and Interpretability Matter

Imagine using a fancy new kitchen appliance that creates delicious dishes, but you have no idea why or how it works. This is similar to using a black box model - it delivers results, but you can't understand the reasoning behind them. Explainability and interpretability aim to shed light on this mystery:

- **Explainability:** This refers to understanding the rationale behind a model's decision-making process. In RAG's case, this means knowing why it generated a specific response to a question or how it arrived at a particular creative text format. Explainability builds trust and allows users to understand the model's thought process.
- **Interpretability:** This dives deeper, aiming to gain insights into the internal workings of the model. Interpretability helps researchers

identify which parts of the model are most influential in generating a particular output. This allows for debugging potential biases or pinpointing areas for improvement within the model itself.

Unveiling the Inner Workings: Techniques for Explainability

While achieving perfect explainability for complex models is an ongoing area of research, here are some techniques being explored for RAG:

- **Attention Analysis:** This technique examines which parts of the input data the model paid most attention to when generating its response. Think of it like identifying the most highlighted ingredients in a recipe to understand what contributed most to the final dish. By analyzing attention weights within the model, researchers can get clues about the reasoning behind RAG's outputs.

Here's a conceptual code example (illustrative) to show a simplified attention analysis snippet:

Python

```python
def         analyze_attention(model, input_data, output):
    """
```

This function analyzes the attention weights of a RAG model to understand

which parts of the input data were most important for generating the output.

Args:

model: The RAG model to be analyzed.

input_data: The data the model was given as input.

output: The output generated by the model.

Returns:

A dictionary containing information about the attention weights for

different parts of the input data.
"""

```
    # ... (implementation details for attention analysis)


    return attention_weights
```

This is a simplified example, of course. Real-world implementations might involve visualizing attention weights or using them to highlight relevant sections of the input data.

- **Feature Ablation:** This technique involves temporarily removing parts of the model's input and observing how the output changes. Think of it like removing ingredients from a recipe one by one to see how it affects the final dish. By analyzing these changes, researchers can gain insights into how different parts of the model contribute to the overall output.

Explainability is an evolving field, and new techniques are constantly being developed. As RAG models become more explainable, they'll gain wider trust and adoption for various applications.

9.2 Addressing Limitations: Fairness, Bias, and Factual Consistency - Building Trustworthy RAG Models

RAG models hold immense potential, but like any powerful tool, they come with limitations. Researchers are actively addressing these limitations, particularly regarding fairness, bias, and factual consistency, to ensure RAG models are trustworthy and reliable.

Why Fairness and Factual Consistency Matter

Imagine a recipe that uses expired ingredients or has steps in the wrong order. The resulting dish might be unpleasant or even unsafe. Similarly, biased or factually inconsistent RAG models can generate misleading or unfair outputs. Let's break down these limitations:

- **Bias:** Training data can harbor hidden biases that a model might inadvertently learn. For example, a biased dataset could lead a RAG model to generate stereotypical content. Mitigating bias is crucial for ensuring fair and responsible use of RAG models.

- **Factual Consistency:** RAG excels at finding relevant information, but ensuring the information it uses and the text it generates are factually accurate is essential. Imagine a RAG model providing incorrect medical advice based on misleading information it retrieved. Factual consistency is paramount for applications where trustworthiness is critical.

Combating Bias: Techniques for Fair RAG Models

Researchers are exploring various techniques to mitigate bias in RAG models:

- **Debiasing Algorithms:** These algorithms can identify and remove potential biases from training datasets. Think of it like carefully cleaning and sorting your ingredients before cooking to ensure there are no unwanted elements.

- **Diverse Training Data:** Using a wider range of training data that reflects the diversity of the real world can help reduce bias in the model. Imagine using a variety of fresh ingredients from different sources to create a well-rounded dish.

Here's a conceptual code snippet (illustrative) to show a simplified debiasing step:

Python

```python
def debias_data(data):
    """
```

This function attempts to identify and remove potential biases from a dataset.

Args:

data: The data to be debiased.

Returns:

A debiased version of the data.

```
"""



    # ... (implementation details for debiasing)



    return debiased_data
```

This is a simplified example. Real-world debiasing techniques might involve sophisticated algorithms for identifying and mitigating bias in text data.

Ensuring Factual Consistency: Building Reliable RAG Models

Techniques are being explored to improve the factual consistency of RAG outputs:

- **Fact-Checking:** Integrating fact-checking mechanisms can help identify and correct factual errors before the model generates its response. Imagine double checking your recipe against a reliable source to ensure you haven't missed any important steps.

- **Knowledge Base Integration:** Connecting RAG models to knowledge bases filled with verified information can provide them with a reliable source of factual data to ground their responses. Think of having a trusted cookbook on hand to consult while following a recipe.

Here's a code snippet (illustrative) for a basic fact-checking step:

Python

```python
def fact_check(text, knowledge_base):
    """
```

This function checks a piece of text against a knowledge base to identify

potential factual inconsistencies.

Args:

text: The text to be fact-checked.

knowledge_base: A database containing factual information.

Returns:

A list of potential factual inconsistencies found in the text.

    """

    # ... (implementation details for fact-checking)

    return factual_inconsistencies

This is a simplified example. Real-world fact-checking might involve sophisticated techniques like named entity recognition and verification against external knowledge sources.

By addressing these limitations, researchers are making RAG models more reliable and trustworthy, ensuring they become valuable tools for various applications.

9.3 The Potential Impact of RAG on Various Industries and Applications: A Glimpse into a RAG-infused Future

RAG technology is like a versatile kitchen appliance with the potential to revolutionize various industries. Its ability to process information, generate creative text formats, and answer questions in an informative way opens doors to a future filled with innovative applications. Here's a glimpse into how RAG might transform different sectors:

Education:

- **Personalized Learning Experiences:** Imagine intelligent tutors powered by RAG that can tailor their teaching styles to individual students' needs. RAG could analyze a student's strengths and weaknesses, then generate customized practice problems or explanations to help them excel.

- **AI-powered Writing Companions:** Struggling students might find support in RAG-based writing assistants. These companions could analyze drafts, suggest improvements, and help with grammar and clarity, fostering stronger writing skills.

Customer Service:

- **Intelligent Chatbots:** Imagine call centers staffed by chatbots that can understand complex questions and requests. RAG-powered chatbots could troubleshoot issues, answer customer inquiries, and even provide personalized recommendations, leading to a more efficient and satisfying customer service experience.

- **Multilingual Support:** RAG's ability to process information in multiple languages could bridge communication gaps. Imagine a customer service chatbot that can seamlessly translate between languages, ensuring all customers receive the support they need regardless of their native language.

Content Creation:

- **Writer's Muse:** RAG can be a boon for writers, overcoming writer's block and sparking creativity. Imagine feeding RAG a starting line or concept and having it generate creative text formats like poems, scripts, or even story outlines, providing writers with a springboard for their imaginations.

- **Research Assistant Extraordinaire:** RAG can be a powerful research companion. Imagine feeding it a broad topic and having it delve into vast amounts of information, summarizing key findings, and even suggesting new research avenues to explore.

Scientific Discovery:

- **Literature Analysis Powerhouse:** Scientific research often involves sifting through mountains of academic papers. RAG could analyze this literature, identify research trends, and generate summaries of relevant findings, expediting the scientific discovery process.

- **Hypothesis Generation on Steroids:** Imagine RAG being used to analyze existing research and generate new hypotheses to be explored. This could open doors to unforeseen breakthroughs and advancements in various scientific fields.

These are just a few examples, and the possibilities are constantly expanding as RAG technology evolves. As researchers continue to address limitations and explore new applications, RAG has the potential to become a transformative force across industries, shaping the future of how we learn, work, and interact with information.

Chapter 10: Conclusion: Mastering RAG for the Future of AI

We've embarked on a journey through the exciting world of RAG, exploring its capabilities and delving into its potential applications. Now, as we reach the final chapter, it's time to tie things together, recapping the key concepts and techniques, pondering the ethical considerations, and envisioning how RAG might shape the future of AI.

10.1 Recap of Key Concepts and Advanced RAG Techniques: Your RAG Chef's Toolkit

Remember that feeling of accomplishment after mastering a complex recipe? Well, consider this chapter your chance to savor the key ingredients and advanced techniques you've learned throughout this RAG journey. Let's refresh your memory and solidify your understanding of the tools in your RAG chef's toolkit:

Foundational Elements: The Building Blocks of RAG

- **RAG Architecture:** We started by diving into the core

Retriever-Augmenter-Generat or (RAG) architecture. This is the backbone of the system, with each component playing a crucial role:

- **Retriever:** This acts like your sous chef, efficiently fetching relevant information from a vast knowledge base based on your query. Imagine searching a well-stocked pantry to find the perfect ingredients for your dish.

- **Augmenter:** Think of this as the creative ingredient mixer. It processes the retrieved information, extracts key elements, and potentially transforms it in a way that prepares it for the generator. In the kitchen, this might involve cleaning, chopping, or even combining ingredients in a specific way.

- **Generator:** This is the star chef, wielding the power of language models. It takes the processed information from the augmenter and uses it to generate the final output, like a well-crafted dish. This could be an answer to a question, a response in a conversation, or even a creative text format.

Advanced Techniques: Taking Your RAG Dishes to the Next Level

We explored how RAG goes beyond the basics, venturing into exciting applications:

- **Question Answering Systems with Supercharged Accuracy:** Imagine a highly informed waiter who not only answers your questions about the menu (factual accuracy) but can also explain the dishes in detail and suggest pairings based on your preferences (contextual understanding). This is what RAG-powered Q&A systems can achieve by combining retrieved information with text generation capabilities.

- **Conversational Chatbots that are More Than Pre-programmed Responses:** Ever feel like you're talking to a wall with a chatbot? RAG chatbots can transform the experience. Imagine a conversational partner that understands the context of your conversation, retrieves relevant information dynamically, and generates informative responses that keep the dialogue flowing naturally.

- **Creative Text Generation: From Brainstorming Buddy to**

Story Writer: Feeling stuck on a writing project? RAG can be your creative sous chef, providing prompts, generating different narrative branches, or even mimicking writing styles. Think of it as a brainstorming partner or a tool to explore different creative avenues.

Remember, these are just a few examples. The possibilities with RAG are constantly expanding as researchers explore new techniques and applications.

By understanding these core concepts and advanced techniques, you've equipped yourself with a solid foundation for using RAG and exploring its potential in your own projects. Now, let's move on to the responsible use of RAG, considering the ethical considerations that come with such a powerful tool.

10.2 The Ethical Considerations of Using RAG Responsibly: Wielding the Power of AI with Care

Imagine a kitchen appliance that can cook delicious meals but has the potential to create a mess if not used properly. Similarly, RAG models are powerful tools, but ethical considerations need to be addressed to ensure responsible use. Let's explore some key points to keep in mind:

1. Bias Mitigation: Ensuring Fairness in the Digital Kitchen

Training data is the foundation for any AI model, and RAG is no exception. The challenge? Training data can harbor hidden biases that a model might inadvertently learn. Imagine using a cookbook with outdated or prejudiced recipes. The resulting dishes might be unfair or unrepresentative. Here's how we can mitigate bias in RAG:

- **Debiasing Algorithms:** These algorithms act like meticulous recipe testers, identifying and removing potential biases from the training data. Think of carefully reviewing your cookbook to ensure the instructions and ingredients are inclusive and avoid perpetuating stereotypes.

- **Diverse Training Data:** Just like a well-stocked pantry with ingredients from various cultures, using a wider range of training data that reflects the diversity of the real world can help reduce bias in the model. Imagine incorporating recipes from various cuisines to create a more well-rounded cookbook for your RAG model.

2. Factual Consistency: Serving Up Truthful Text

RAG excels at finding relevant information, but ensuring the information it uses and the text it generates are factually accurate is crucial. Imagine a recipe website accidentally recommending expired ingredients. The results could be disastrous! Here's how to ensure RAG serves up factual accuracy:

- **Fact-Checking:** Think of this as a double-checking mechanism, like verifying ingredients and expiration dates before you start cooking. Fact-checking techniques can help identify and correct factual errors before the RAG model generates its response.

- **Knowledge Base Integration:** Imagine having a trusted encyclopedia of culinary knowledge readily available while following a recipe. Connecting RAG models to knowledge bases filled with verified information can provide them with a reliable source of factual data to ground their responses.

3. Transparency and Explainability: Demystifying the RAG Chef's Process

RAG models can be complex, and understanding how they arrive at their conclusions is essential for trust and responsible use. Imagine a recipe that only lists ingredients but provides no instructions. It would be difficult to replicate the dish successfully! Here's how we can make RAG models more transparent:

- **Explainability Techniques:** These techniques are like revealing the chef's secret ingredients and cooking methods. They aim to understand the rationale behind a model's decision-making process. For RAG, this might involve analyzing attention weights to see which parts of the retrieved information were most influential in generating the output.

- **Human Oversight:** Ultimately, a human chef with culinary expertise oversees the kitchen. Similarly, human oversight is crucial for RAG applications. Humans should be involved in setting parameters, monitoring outputs, and ensuring the model is used responsibly.

By keeping these ethical considerations in mind, we can ensure that RAG is used for good, promoting fairness, factual accuracy, and transparency as we weave the future of AI. In the next chapter, we'll explore how RAG might contribute to this exciting future.

10.3 A Glimpse into the Future: How RAG Will Shape the Next Generation of AI

Fast forward a few years from now. Imagine a world where AI seamlessly integrates into our lives, not just as tools but as collaborators. This future is where RAG technology has the potential to shine. Let's delve into how RAG might revolutionize the way we interact with AI:

1. Human-AI Collaboration: A Powerful Symphony

RAG can bridge the gap between humans and machines, fostering a **symphonic**

collaboration. Imagine an orchestra conductor who can not only play instruments but can also understand the composer's intent and guide the ensemble towards a harmonious performance:

- **AI Assistants That Augment Human Capabilities:** Imagine RAG-powered intelligent assistants that can anticipate your needs, provide relevant information dynamically, and even complete routine tasks. Think of a research assistant who can not only find scientific papers but can also summarize key findings and suggest new research avenues.

- **Creative Partners That Spark Innovation:** RAG can be a muse for artists and writers, overcoming creative block and generating new ideas. Imagine a composer who can collaborate with a RAG model to explore different musical styles and create unique compositions.

2. Democratization of AI: Making Powerful Technology More Accessible

RAG's modular architecture and ongoing research hold the potential to **democratize AI**. Imagine a world where AI technology is no longer limited to large corporations and research labs:

- **Accessible Tools for Developers:** RAG's modular nature makes it adaptable for various applications. This, along with advancements in user-friendly development tools, could enable a wider range of developers to leverage RAG's capabilities. Think of open-source RAG libraries that make it easier for developers to integrate RAG functions into their applications.
- **More Inclusive AI Development:** By making AI development more accessible, we can encourage a wider range of voices and perspectives to

contribute to the field. This can lead to the creation of AI models that are more representative of the real world and less susceptible to bias.

3. The Future of AI Applications: A World of Possibilities

RAG's ability to process information and generate human-like text paves the way for a future filled with groundbreaking AI applications across various sectors:

- **Education:** Imagine personalized learning experiences tailored to individual student needs, with RAG-powered tutors providing targeted instruction and feedback.

- **Healthcare:** Envision AI-powered medical assistants that can understand patient symptoms, access vast medical knowledge bases, and even communicate with doctors in real-time to improve diagnosis and treatment planning.

- **Scientific Discovery:** Imagine RAG models that can analyze scientific data from telescopes or microscopes, identify patterns and anomalies, and formulate new hypotheses to accelerate scientific progress.

- **Content Creation:** Consider a future where RAG helps create educational materials, marketing copy, or even scripts for films and television shows, freeing up human creativity for higher-level tasks.

The future of AI is bright, and RAG is poised to play a leading role. As researchers continue to refine RAG's capabilities and address ethical considerations, we can expect to see even more innovative applications emerge, shaping a future where humans and AI work together to solve complex problems and create a better world.

www.ingramcontent.com/pod-product-compliance
Lightning Source LLC
Chambersburg PA
CBHW071242050326
40690CB00011B/2224